How I See God in Autism

Travis Breeding

Copyright © 2014 Travis Breeding

All rights reserved.

ISBN: **1500398624**
ISBN-13: **978-1500398620**

DEDICATION

I dedicate this book to God. God is Good: All the Time. All the time: God is Good.

Amen

Let everything that has breath praise the lord.

Amen

Psalm 150:13

ACKNOWLEDGMENTS

Thank you God for all you do and for guiding me through the journey with my faith.

HOW I SEE GOD IN AUTISM

There are not many books out there about Autism and faith. How does God play a role in someone with Autism's life? This is an area that can be touchy for many individuals living with Autism. We live in a society where anyone who is different or appears to be different is often judged by others. Sometimes this includes being judged by people in places in which one would assume you would find the most acceptance and love.

As a child growing up I struggled greatly with fitting in at school and making friends with my peers. I can remember how I would get excited as a little boy just waiting on the weekend to get here because I would not have to go to school and face all of the social struggles I had with the other children. As a little kid Sunday school class was a lot of fun and I felt accepted there. I felt as if I belonged. I remember one of my favorite songs being "Jesus Loves the Little Children" Red and Yellow, black and white, they are precious in his sight.

I grew up believing in that. I loved church and even had the chance to participate in a lot of church events. My favorite aspect of church was participating on the worship team. I loved using my talent as a trombone player to worship the lord and help lead others in worship. We are all blessed with some kind of amazing talent that God provides for us. When we make the choice to use that talent to give back to God and glorify his name there are so many good things that happen.

Throughout my childhood I was a very quiet little boy. No one really knew that I had the desire to interact with others because I kept it very hidden. I was not intentionally trying to hide this great desire within side me but I was hiding it out of fear. The fear was born in the fact that I did not understand how to interact with other children. I knew that the other kids knew how to interact with each other but I could not see how this works. I could just see the other kids sharing in laughter and games and so desperately on the inside.

As a child even as young as seven or eight years old I projected that I was happy. I gave off the perception that I did not have the desire to make friends or even have friends. Others would just often assume that I was a loner and wanted to be a loner but that was not the case at all. I simply did not understand social interaction or how to connect with others.

To this day this is a great struggle for me. It was not until I was diagnosed with Asperger Syndrome at age 22 that I began to understand what some of the issues I was dealing with were.

Truthfully life was a lot less hectic for me when I did not have this desire to have friendships or relationships in my life I find that God does not judge me for being autistic and for that I am very grateful. As a child I had a relationship with two people or things in my life. I was close with God and I was close with my trombone.

Playing trombone had become a special interest of mine. It was a coping mechanism that I used to help me deal with all of the social isolation, depression, and loneliness. If it had not been for God and the ability to excel at the trombone I am not sure I would have survived high school without killing myself.

There were many times when I just wanted to give up I was two completely different people. On the outside I was this happy teenager who had a lot going for him. I was involved in a lot of music groups at my school and my church. On the outside it appeared as if I had many friends because I was so involved with music that the other musicians who were acquaintances would appear to be my friends.

Yes, I would often spend time hanging out with the other musicians during a band practice for school or an orchestra practice at the church, but when the rehearsals were over and the other kids congregated in groups to go out to Taco Bell or Pizza Hut I did not connect. I went home to lock myself in my room and spend the evening alone and all by myself with my trombone.

On the inside I was a distressed teenager who was lost in a society that doesn't understand someone or something that is different. On the inside I knew I was different than my neurotpyical peers who did not have Autism. (At the time I did not know that I had autism or even fully understand what it is.) Autism was something I knew of but it is amazing how much a person's definition of Autism can change when you begin to fully understand the disorder. The truth is, it is so much more than just being non-verbal and unable to communicate.

On the inside I was an emotional mess but I was not able to communicate those distressed emotions to anyone on the outside. It can be hard to really help someone dealing with depression or serious mental health issues if the person is unable to communicate or relate to others. You actually need the ability to have close friendships and relationships with other individuals so that they could even have a chance to be able to pick up on some of the emotions being displayed by the distressed individual.

This created a situation in which I was just waiting to explode. I was going to have a serious psychotic break if I did not receive help or intervention to treat my social issues. By the time I was 20 I could tell that I was becoming mental ill on top of all of my social issues.

A person with Autism will typically have a high IQ. This meant that I was able to tell exactly what was going on. I understood what mental illness was and I began to comprehend for the first time at about the age of 20 that I had a serious mental health problem. I picked up on the mental health problem long before I knew that I was autistic. In fact, it was in discovering that I had some serious mental health issues that I was able to learn that I had autism. Had it not been for the psychotic break and the mental health issues that began to present themselves in my life I am unsure if I would have ever had the chance to learn that I was indeed autistic.

I might have been okay if I would have been able to stay in high school for the rest of my life. Music was definitely my coping mechanism for the issues I was dealing with. I hid my mental illnesses and social issues in the ability to excel in music and participate in several musical groups within my high school and community. There's truth to the whole concept of music therapy. It can be a gift from God and it was a gift from God that I used to my advantage for several years in my childhood.

After high school it was like I had to start over. Everything that was already in place for me structurally at the high school level was taken away from me when I walked across that stage and shook the school board member's hand to receive my high school diploma. Everything I had grown to know and be comfortable with was about to be stolen from me with one walk across a stage and a hand shake. I was about to begin a brand new life on a college campus. I was about to go from what I thought was a big high school of 2100 kids to a university of over 60,000 students. Yikes!

It would be the next seven years of life that would create a near tragedy. A tragedy in which I would almost kill myself. I would endure several suicide attempts over the first few years of my 20's. Thankfully I have survived those and now my goal is to prevent others from going through the same things as me.

Perhaps the most heartbreaking tragedy for me was when I almost lost my faith in God . God never did anything to me to make me lose my faith in him. It was more the reactions I received form some of God's people that made me doubt my faith.

Feeling lost and confused as a teenager at the age of 19 on a new college campus in Bloomington, Indiana I decided to leave that school and go to a smaller college where there would be many less students. I was so overwhelmed with the number of students at Indiana University in Bloomington that I would cry myself to sleep every night. The music school itself was nearly as big as my entire high school.

I transferred to Indiana Wesleyan University in Marion Indiana at the age of 19 and decided to begin my college career that way. I felt much better about this opportunity because it was a much smaller campus and I actually had a music professor at Indiana Wesleyan that I knew very well because he was a teacher of mine in junior high school. Surely this would be a much greater and easier experience for me than going to Indiana University in Bloomington?

This is a series I am starting about Christianity, Faith, God, and Autism. In order to fully understand the rest of this serious I ask that you read a little about Autism. It is helpful to have some background on Autism and how it can affect someone's social life. In the next section of this book you will learn more about what it is like to be Autistic. Then in book II I will begin to discuss my faith and how I almost lost it during my experience at Indiana Wesleyan University. Then later on in the series I will discuss how I am finding my faith again now in life. I fully believe in God and he does so many amazing things for me in my life. I want to share about how God has helped me cope with Autism and even began helping me to overcome many of the social issues that I face in dealing with autism. This next section will give you some background on Autism. Thank you for taking an interest in learning.

AUTISM

I remember the day I was diagnosed with Asperger's Syndrome like it was yesterday. October 30th 2007. I was scared and felt alone. I wasn't sure what to do after leaving the doctor's office.

I can imagine you are feeling many mixed emotions as you are raising your son or daughter. I want to provide some encouragement for you. Now, 28 years old, nearly 6 years after being diagnosed with Asperger's Syndrome; I am the happiest I have ever been in my life.

My goal in life is to help you the parent or teacher gain better insight into what living with Autism is like. I want to help you help your children or student. I have published 12 books about growing up with Autism. I like to speak about life with autism whenever I get the chance. I am independent. I live in my own apartment and drive a car.

Be encouraged that your child can achieve all of this and more. I want to tell you Congratulations. You have a very special child.

I want to share this E-book with you. This is a brief overview of Autism the way I see it, feel it, and experience it. This is an overview of what you will see in the rest of my books. I hope you find this helpful in relating to your child or student. Happy reading.

In the following section, you'll find an appendix of terms and explanations of things dealing with Asperger's Syndrome. These are topics that were introduced throughout the book and all are related to Autism. I wanted to expand upon some things at the end of the book. This is a great source for a greater explanation of Asperger's Syndrome.

The Reason behind the Special Interest

There are a couple of reasons as to why the special interest develops to such an intense level in an individual on the autism spectrum. I should note that this is only my opinion and you should always consult a professional, but I do believe that getting advice from someone who's experienced this can be very insightful.

Reason Number One

The child on the spectrum doesn't have a normal level of social skills that is up to par with their peers.

I formed a special interest in things because I didn't have the capability to carry on a conversation about things that other kids might have wanted to talk about. This caused me to be excluded from any group of students who was ever congregating or sitting around, talking. When one is excluded from a group, what's left for him to do?

Throughout middle and high school, I would often sit at home and just think about music, practice my trombone nonstop, and listen to jazz recordings to the point to where it became an obsession but also a way to not feel so lonely.

For me, music- and in particular the trombone- was my best friend. I had pretty much lost my best friend. To me, music was my best friend. It was what I liked and it was easy to interact with. There were no social norms or rules to follow to be friends with the music.

The special interest is also something that doesn't go away. People come and go, but things are usually always here and consistent. For a person with Autism or Asperger's Syndrome, losing a friend who's a person can be devastating-not only because we become attached to the person but also because of our lack of ability to make friends. So when we lose a friend, we have to try to make new friends, and this is very stressful for us. I cannot speak for all people with an autism diagnosis, but I can tell you that I'm one who ants friends. I've always wanted to be included in the group. I know that there are some people on the spectrum who don't have an interest in having friendships at all or interacting with others. Then there are some who do but can't talk or communicate in any way at all, which would be extremely frustrating.

To sum things up, the special interest forms because the person with autism is excluded from basically all forms of social interaction by their peers. Without having any social interaction at all, they have a lot of time on their hands, and they spend that time doing something they like. It's just that they spend more time with the thing they are interested in rather than being around other people, which causes the interest to become a friend. In my opinion, the special interest is something that someone on the spectrum uses to cope with not being able to build successful relationships with other people. Because they can't have a friend, they replace the friend with the special interest.

Reason Number 2

Communicating with the special interest is easy and much less stressful than communicating with an NT.

A lot of people just don't realize how stressful and tiring talking to people can be for individuals on the spectrum. It's extremely hard to talk to someone. Just trying to look them in the eye and say hi is a challenge for most of us. Therefore, it is stressful. It's also so much work that it can become tiring. People with autism often report being tired after even just a brief social exchange with someone. This is happening because of the dysfunction in their central nervous system.

It is my opinion that because communication with people is very stressful, challenging, tiring, and yes, frustrating for us on the spectrum that people with autism form a special interest. Think about it. It's so much easier for us to communicate with an object than it is to communicate with a human being. For me, playing trombone comes naturally. I can communicate very well and articulate what I'm saying with it. But when I'm talking to people, I have a hard time communicating. I get misunderstood, and my actions get misinterpreted. I get ridiculed, made fun of, and bullied due to my lack of social understanding and awareness.

When I'm playing my trombone, I can't talk, and I'm not communicating to a person directly. I am communicating to them indirectly by providing a musical sound that they can enjoy. Without having to worry if I'm doing something wrong or unacceptable, I'm able to relax and find much more enjoyment. Even if I was to go bowling in a group or putt-putt golfing, I wouldn't be able to enjoy myself because there is a lot of social interaction expected. So therefore, it's so easy to see why an individual with autism might develop a special interest. Special interests are easy to communicate with, making them virtually stress free. They relieve stress. The individual with autism doesn't have to say anything to them. They don't have to worry about the interest making fun of them or judging them, and they can keep and maintain the relationship at ease for a lifetime.

How do we handle the special interest in an individual with Autism?

I hear a lot of talk from professionals who are frustrated with the special interest. They are frustrated with the special interest because it is hard for them to deal with. It's hard to take away something that is loved by someone so much that it's almost a part of who they are. However, the special interest can cause trouble and be hurtful to the person with autism because they can talk about a subject too much to the point that they overwhelm people. They can lose friendships as a result. As they get older, the special interest or interests can change. Sometimes these can involve other people. For example, it is quite common for an adult with Asperger's Syndrome to develop a special interest in making friends. This is when the interest can become complicated and hard to deal with. Sometimes the interest becomes a fixation with a certain friend leading people to believe the individual with autism is obsessed with the individual. This can be unhealthy to both people. It is also extremely uncomfortable for the person who is the special interest of the individual with autism.

The neurotypical person who wouldn't know much about autism or a special interest would see all of this attention from someone with autism as being borderline obsessive. In this case it is important that we handle the special interest and moderate it as it directly affects other people, but it's also a part of who the person on the autism spectrum really is. So we're in a catch 22 position. We shouldn't change who someone is. But we can't let it affect their interactions with others.

This has been the most frustrating part of my adult life. When making friends, I often heard people say "just be who you are." But then in all reality it's the characteristics of Asperger's Syndrome, such as being clingy or obsessive in social interaction, that scares people away. Those characteristics are a part of who I am. I can't change them m go away. But I can learn to control them and

em as I am doing in my friendship with my best

friend now.

Taking the special interest away is not the only solution. A special interest can possibly be modified or toned down with the proper treatment, but it is hard to completely take it away and make it nonexistent. I can totally understand how you could become frustrated with the individual with the interest, so I have thought about effective ways to handle the person's special interest.

First of all, it's extremely crucial that we remember the special interest is not just an interest. The special interest could actually be the person's best friend. So whenever you think about trying to eliminate an interest, please try to remember that you're not really taking away an interest but a friend the person loves. You're also dealing with more than just a want. You're dealing with more of a need. The special interest could be like a need for survival. It could be the only thing that they have to look forward to in life. Taking it away can lead to severe isolation and depression. It's like a leg for a person without autism. Life would be very difficult if you were to lose your legs. If you take a leg away, what happens? You limp around and maybe get by in life, but with the leg you are able to hop, skip, and run just like everyone else.

What I am getting at here is the special interest in an individual with autism can be his or her best friend. So when you're trying to eliminate the special interest in someone with autism, it's going to be painful and uncomfortable to them. Compare it to losing your wife or a close loved one. Obviously, this is going to cause a lot of discomfort. That could be damaging to the individual. So I suggest that as long as the special interest is completely appropriate, we don't try to eliminate it completely. If it's so intense that it's interfering with the person's lifestyle or lifestyles of anyone around the person, then I propose trying to control the intensity level of a special interest. Taking it away from them completely could be tragic.

What if it's an inappropriate interest?

So what do we do if an interest is inappropriate and disturbing to society? I'm not sure there is a good way to handle a situation like this that we know of yet. I had the opportunity to hear about a wonderful young teenager. He has autism and has developed a special interest in girls' feet. Yes a foot fetish. However, because it's a special interest and not just an interest, the intensity level of the interest is overbearing and inappropriate. More often than not you'll find that a special interest is really just a neruotypical person's interest multiplied in intensity, making it a special interest. This teen will walk up to high school girls and tell them that they have beautiful feet. This may come off as a little creepy to the average high school girl. It is situations like this that have been most frustrating in my life.

To an individual with autism, it can be hard to understand the concept of "creepy." Neurotypicals have this filtering system that recognizes when things are a little off or creepy. It's just a feeling that a neurotypical is able to get from their subconscious level. As someone with autism, I don't get this feeling from anyone and am unable to tell or understand when I am putting out this signalCreepy is frustrating because society has made it out to sound like such a horrible word. When someone says I'm creepy, I automatically feel like I'm a horrible person because I've hurt them in some way. In my mind I think very logically about social situations. To me a lot of social norms and unwritten rules are illogical. I don't understand them. This causes me to make people feel awkward and uncomfortable at times.

One of the things that neurotypicals have an understanding for that I don't is something called "implied meaning." This is a way people communicate with one another without actually saying something. For example, if I call you 25 times today it means something. There's meaning to it. Neurotypicals look for hidden meaning in things and they find it often. Implied meaning is something that I don't understand. How can my actions of me doing something mean something that I haven't verbally told you? I don't get it. But neurotyipcals do.

As I've mentioned, the special interest is like the individuals best friend. So as weird as it might sound, the feet of the girls the teen was interest in are quite possibly like a best friend to him. I have a similar issue with women's arms.

It would be extremely hurtful and tragic to someone with autism if you tried to eliminate the interest in girls' feet entirely. However, there are a couple of options to help diminish how intense it is and how it's affecting those girls who have the beautiful feet.

A special interest can never be eliminated completely. But, it can be controlled. The best way to accomplish this is through Applied Behavioral Analysis, known as ABA therapy in the autism community. The simple definition for ABA therapy is that it's a system of rewards/punishments or take away. When the person complies with a request, they are given positive reinforcement to encourage the chance that they will do it right again and again. The take away is used when the person is unable to comply to a request. Meaning they might not get to play their favorite video game that evening if they didn't meet their goal.

For the guy with the foot interest. We might say "If you can go a day without complimenting girls feet then you can have a reward at the end of the day." If you can't then you won't get to play your favorite video game after school that night.

Another way to approach this would be to try to modify the interest. Notice I said modify, not replace or take away. By modifying it, the person is still able to find enjoyment in the interest but maybe in a different way. Maybe the behavioral consultant could get him to rethink the thought before he says it to a girl.

The consultant should try to get him to not act on his thought so fast. This will allow him time to think and maybe change the thought into something that is more appropriate. If when he has the thought, "Holly has beautiful feet. I'm going to tell her that." We could get him to think and switch to something like, Holly looks really nice today, or Holy is beautiful today, or even, Holly has pretty eyes today, this might come off as a little more appropriate and prevent any tension at school between him and girls. This would make everyone more comfortable with the entire situation.

This is not something that would be easy to do with someone with autism. Trained behavior analyst spend countless hours each week working with children and teens who have autism. It takes an intense approach and a very dedicated therapist to be able to help someone with autism modify behaviors. Applied behavior is in my opinion a gift to the autism community that should be accessed more and covered by more insurance programs.

Importance of Being Able to Escape into Imagination

The ability to escape into imagination is a useful tool for someone who's dealing with Autism or Asperger's Syndrome. I found it to be a way to connect with someone. I used my escape into imagination to connect with actors and actresses in movies. Even though these actors and actresses have no idea who I am, I still feel that I can put on a movie or watch a rerun of Saved by the Bell and connect with these people more than anyone in the world.

It's good for individuals on the spectrum to be able to find this type of connection with someone, even if it is in a make-believe world. Without being able to do this there could be a lot more depression. Let's face it. Having no one at all to communicate with is lonely. Having someone, whether it be an animal or a make-believe character, to connect with could do wonders for people on the spectrum.

As I get older I am finding that I escape into imagination a little less frequently. Even when I do those make-believe imaginary friends aren't the same as having a real friend. I sometimes create little make believe characters in my mind to be friends with. Seth has been one of them. But, Seth is not like real people. He can't really talk back to me. So it's a one sided conversation.

I think as I get older my I'm able to comprehend more that the make-believe world I create in my mind to help cope with Autism isn't real. When I was younger I believed everything in the make believe world was real. With age, I think I have more capability to recognize the difference between real and fake. It is still difficult and sometimes I do go off on a phase where I live in the make-believe world for a few weeks or a month or so. I have to be snapped out of that phase in order to come back to the real world.

Danger of Escaping Into Imagination

While I do believe that being able to escape into imagination is often extremely beneficial to an individual on the spectrum, I also want to caution of the chance of it becoming a dangerous situation. There's a chance of the person escaping into imagination too often. If this were to happen, the person could seclude themselves from the real world. Even though the real world is often a very hurtful place for us on the spectrum to live in, it is necessary for us to return from that state of imagination and get out into the real world and try to do our best at fitting in and making real friends.

It is important that people with Autism continue to seek out therapy options for improving social skill sets and social thinking. If someone stays in that state of imagination for too long they can become comfortable and believe that state of imagination is their real life. They can stop trying to be a participant in the real world and seclude themselves to their own fantasy world. It's important to have a healthy balance here. The fantasy world that they create can be helpful at times but if it's used or accessed too often can become harmful to themselves and to the friendships and relationships in their life.

I definitely understand how painful and unbearable the real world can be to us at times. People with Autism have likely grown up always being accused of doing something wrong or being annoying. With that said, I can not express how important it is that we continue to try and get out in the real world. Put ourselves out there. Continue to seek out friendships and meet new people. The absolute worst thing we can do is seclude ourselves to a life locked inside of our own homes due to fear of the real world. I often meet people with Autism who are trapped in their own world because they quit trying to be a member of the real world. As hard as it is, we've got to keep trying. Feeling trapped is the worst feeling in the world.

There is irony in this as well. When I am in my make-believe world I often cling to my best friend in real life. Because she's the only tie I have left to the real world at that point and time. Because I've became so socially isolated. Texting her, talking to her, and seeing her are the only ties and connections I have to the real world when I'm at this point and time.

The Autism mind is a very fascinating and complex place to be. While I create a "make believe" world to help me cope with the overwhelming real world, my best friend is my only tie to the real world when I'm in that make believe world. For me, creating the make believe world isn't something that I want to do. I don't necessarily want to be there. But I think it's become a natural response or coping tool for when I feel overwhelmed with something real.

How Can we tell if escaping into imagination is becoming too extreme?

There are a couple of things to watch for here. The main thing is watching to see how the person acts at home. If the individual is still socializing with family members, it's likely okay. However, if it gets to the point where the individual doesn't even want to be around his or her family anymore, there is likely a problem.

The problem being that escaping into imagination or that make-believe world has become too comfortable. There's no pain in there. The individual has no motivation to come back into the real world now because they've managed to find a pain-free and predictable environment.

Tony Attwood says it best in his book The Complete Guide to Asperger's Syndrome. When an individual on the spectrum is by themselves, there is no impairment. The impairment doesn't happen until there is another individual with them. So with the people in their own make-believe world, with no other real human beings around, it becomes safe; life becomes easy, as there is no communication to worry about. I couldn't agree more with what Tony said in his book.

Another way you could catch that this is becoming a problem is if you're able to listen to the individual talk when they're around you. If you feel that they're constantly talking about it like it's becoming their special interest, then it's time to step in and try to modify the make believe world and how it's used.

What is the best way to correct the interest?

There is no clear-cut one size fits all answer. There's not a simple way to bring someone out of their make-believe world and back to the real world. For me, I've had to learn the hard way many times. Many times my make believe world has pushed people away.

This almost happened with my real best friend. Last summer I had this make believe world created where I believed that my best friend was my mother. By continually interacting with her like she was my mother and believing that to be true, I started pushing her away.

I don't think there would have been a good way to come back to reality. I find in most cases with the make believe world for me, I have to be slapped in the face with reality in order to fall out of the make-believe world and find my way back to the real world.

In this case it took my friend being very frustrated after being very patient and understanding saying she couldn't do it anymore. She just couldn't be my mom and couldn't be a part of my make believe world any longer. It was like a wake up call. I knew I had to somehow gain control over my thoughts and come back to reality in order to save the friendship I had with my best friend. It's those real life wake up calls that I think we will find bring people with Autism back into the real world from their own make-believe fantasy world.

Correcting this situation can be very painful for the individual with Autism. Because a make –believe world has become a place of comfort and security, taking that security blanket away will not be easy to do. Please allow time. Giving someone who is on the Autism spectrum time to adjust or time to change something or time do do anything is the best gift that you could ever give them. Often, if the individual is given enough time, they will comply with the request. They just need more time and patience to comply with your request. It takes us longer to process changes.

Giving an Ample Amount of Time for an Individual on the Spectrum to Comply

If you are working with children or young adults on the Autism Spectrum working to correct or modify behaviors, you really need patience. People often expected me to adapt to change or fix something in an instant, without giving me a chance to practice or internalize the thought. This became extremely frustrating for me. I often see people who are so inpatient with each other, but time is something that the individual on the spectrum needs. They need to be able to process your request and then think about it for just a little longer than the average individual who is NT.

I bet if someone were to do a study on people who were on the Autism Spectrum, they would find nearly all, if not all, were able to comply with a request to change a behavior if they were given an ample amount of time.

Physical and Emotional Abuse

For an individual on the Autism spectrum, there can be many things that can present a danger for them. Depending on the severity of the autism, the dangers could range from not being socially aware and making social mistakes or going as far as doing something that's dangerous and could cause them to get hurt or worse. These individuals on the spectrum are just simply not aware of the many dangers of the world. I know for me this has been very much the case through my entire life. I would be easily taken advantage of. Therefore it's crucial that we are aware of this information and can hopefully come up with a way of preventing someone with Autism from being put into harmful, dangerous, uncomfortable situations.

The Friendship/Acquaintance Ratio

It was my junior year. I had no idea about the friendship/acquaintance ratio then. I didn't know what it was or that it even existed. It's actually something I came up with about three or four years ago that I've used as a way of explaining my social interactiosn with people. I often tried extremely hard to develop peer relationships. It seemed like the harder I would try to develop a relationship or friendship with someone the more they would hate me or think I was creepy or psycho. Obviously now I'm aware that they didn't hate me, they were just uncomfortable with me or my behaviors towards them.

The friendship/acquaintance ratio is a relationship between an individual with Autism and a neurotypical. The individual with Autism or Asperger's Syndrome is trying so hard to develop a friendship with the NT that it's an imbalanced equation or ratio.

To the individual on the spectrum, as soon as an NT individual so much as says hi to us and or smiles at us, the NT has become our best friend. While, the NT individual was just saying hi to be friendly and might not even be interested in learning the person on the spectrum's name.

The neurotypical individuals have established a social network that is full of many different people at all different levels of the friendship circle. They have guys that are friends and girls that are friends. Some of them have best friends or acquaintances. Others have co-workers and even more casual friends in that circle as well.

To the neurotypical, meeting the new person won't mean anything at all to them. It will just be "someone they met while they were out and about that night in most cases." Chances are the next day they wouldn't even remember your name or anything about you. Most people have their network of friends established.

The individual with Autism doesn't understand this, and even if he or she did, they still would have a hard time with it because it just makes them feel so good that they didn't get ignored or even worse. The fact that someone actually smiles at me and says hi to me makes me feel good. It never happened much in my past and so when it does I gravitate to it because I really want friends. My reaction is to make that person my best friend right away. The instant they smile or say hi, they can be my best friend.

Because the neurotypical has years of knowing and understanding how to develop friendships appropriately they know that it takes time. They aren't in a rush to bring someone new into their life. I feel a part of this is due to the fact that they themselves have been hurt in friendships and relationships by other neurotypicals.

You see, a common mistake that I made in my younger days with Autism is believing that I was the only one who had trouble making friends or got hurt by other people. I didn't realize that neurotypicals actually can get hurt by other neurotypicals as well. The idea didn't make sense to me. I had this image in my brain that all neurotypicals were amazing and wonderful people that I wanted to be like. As it turns out this simply just isn't the case.

So what happens is that the NT person becomes the person on the spectrum's best friend instantly, while to the NT individual the person on the spectrum just becomes an acquaintance. (Someone they might or might not have an interest in seeing again.)

Due to the excitement in the person on the spectrum, they will become overly anxious and want to develop a friendship with the NT individual more quickly than the NT is comfortable with. This will cause the NT to accuse or assume that the individual on the spectrum is being disrespectful and purposely missing these cues or common knowledge about building a friendship that NT's come preprogrammed with. The person on the spectrum might end up calling the NT too much or too often or texting and e-mailing them too much. They can become overbearing to the NT individual, and they will retreat and try to get rid of the individual on the spectrum.

This is something that has happened to me time and time again. When you end up getting rejected or made fun of, you can't understand because you just don't realize or comprehend what you've done wrong. For me, even when someone would explain it to me, it wouldn't make much sense, and I just couldn't understand why they were reacting that way to me. An example would be with texting. I don't understand how it could be possible to text someone too much. There is nothing harmful about a text message, un less you are saying mean things in it. But if I'm texting someone and I send three hundred nice messages per day, I don't see how this can bother them or upset them. I just don't comprehend it. I feel as if they punish me because I'm nice to them and text them too much in their eyes but I don't understand how or why it's too much. It doesn't register in my brain.

SOCIAL THINKING AND CONTEXT (Imporant Autism Guide)

Education of children on the autism spectrum presents a challenge because of our literal interpretation of things and the fact that no two social situations are exactly the same. The context to each situation may be completely different. For example, having small talk at the library with a friend is unlike having small talk at a sporting event or concert. There are differences involved in how you would have conversation. One is a very quiet environment and the other is a loud environment. Other's body language will also be completely different at the two events.

Dr. Peter Gerhardt says "Context is King." This is one of the biggest and most important things we can teach. It holds true with every situation when teaching social skills. When teaching a child a skill like toiletry skills it's very important to talk about context. We have to teach how to use the restroom in a safe manner that is proper for the current situation. We must distinguish between restroom rules at home in our private bathroom to the restroom rules used in a public restroom.

However, when sexuality is involved this can be the difference between safe and unsafe. Good outcome or negative consequences.

Some people on the autism spectrum struggle with understanding the context of social situations. A perfect example of this is when a 26 year old woman got pregnant. Her behaviour therapist asked her why she wasn't using birth control. She said that she was. She was right according to her knowledge base and the way she understood the context of the situation.

The issue was that her mom told her she couldn't get pregnant until she was married. With the literal interpretation people on the spectrum had she really believed that she couldn't physically get pregnant until she was married.

We have to teach literal interpretation and context from an early age. If not we'll see negative consequences and a preventable situation will occur.

It's also important to convey to your children that their peers don't always know everything and may try and mislead them. I've had guys my age try and give me advice about talking to women before. They would sometimes tell me things to say to a girl that ended up being completely inappropriate. They weren't exactly trying to help me they wanted to have some fun and new I was gullible so they gave me bad advice that at best got me laughed at by both the guys and the girls, at worst could have gotten me into huge trouble.

Here are a couple examples of what other guys have told me to do.

Example 1

If you like her go up to her and grab her. Say, "Hey baby, what's up?"

Example 2

Go up to her and tell her you want to stick it in her.

I was receiving horrible advice. It wasn't because the other guys didn't know what to say or do it was because they knew I was naïve on the subject and would do anything to figure out how to get a girlfriend. The thing I want to convey is that this didn't just happen in middle school and high school. Grown men in their 20's would tell me this stuff when I was out trying to meet people and make friends. If your child doesn't fully know or understand appropriate from inappropriate they could find themselves in a very uncomfortable and even dangerous situation.

It is very important that you are open with the issue of sexuality with your children from a young age. If you can talk about it with them and they gain respect for you then they'll be more likely to listen to your guidelines and follow them. If you haven't had these discussions with your child and they start going to their peers to figure it they could be severely miss led or taken advantage of. I can't comply enough how important it is that we have these sexuality education talks with children from the earliest age possible.

Someone with autism needs to be taught that while there's a general idea of what behaviour is expected in society because of different contexts the rules fluctuate some from situation to situation. As parents and therapist we can not just teach a general rule and expect them to be able to get through life with no speed bumps. When teaching a kid how to approach a group of people we can't just teach him by role playing in the office setting. We also can't just go to the library and teach him either. We need to be sure that we're teaching him how to approach and introduce himself to people at school, work, the library, a museum, the supermarket and more. You can see why this is such a daunting task. It's hard work and won't be easy for you, your child, or your child's therapist but it's work that must be done. It's something I wish I would have learned as a kid growing up rather than trying to teach myself as an adult. It's a challenge but if you want your kid to be safe and happy it's important we do this.

Contrary to what someone may say social skills are not a simple thing to learn or teach. Social skills are complex. It will take a lot more than saying this is how you do this. I've found getting advice from other neurotypicals my age is a bad idea because they simply just don't know how they use the skill they're using. Most social skills are unlearned. A teacher never sat in the classroom having a lesson on approaching a group of people and engaging them in conversation. She was trying to keep the class quiet so she could teach.

My brain works like an on/off switch with social skills. I either get it or I don't. This also means I either really like someone a lot or I'm not interested in them. This is troublesome because people tend to have different categories of friends. Some categories might be

Acquaintance

Casual friend

Co-worker

Good friend

Best friend

Significant other

I typically go straight from acquaintance to best friend or significant other. I was never taught the in between steps of the friendship building process. This causes me to come on too strong and overwhelm the other person on the receiving end of my attention. This type of behaviour is inappropriate in our society and therefore others were associating me with the inappropriate behaviour. I had to change this so I began to get to work on social skills.

Here's an example of the process of using a urinal in the men's restroom. Most of us would just walk right in take care of business and be done with it. However, for those of us with autism who didn't naturally pick up on how to use the urinal properly we must go through a detailed step by step process.

1. Walk in the restroom.

2. Do not look at anyone.

3. Stand in line if there is one.

4. Behave appropriately in line.

5. Choose the proper Urinal when available.

6. Keep eyes straight forward.

7. Avoid being next to someone if possible.

8. Definitely avoid being next to two people.

9. Unzip your pants.

10. Aim properly

11. zip your pants

12. Flush the Urinal

13. Go to the Sink

14. Turn the water on

15. Wash your hands

16. Put soap on your hands

17. wrinse your hands

18. turn water off

19. dry hands with paper towel or blow dryer

20. exit the restroom

Not many of us would realize that there would be 20 steps involved in just using the men's room urinal. Look at how complex of a skill this is. If you just tell your kid to go in and use the restroom who knows what may happen in there. If their behaviour is not socially appropriate it could lead to making others feel uncomfortable. This will cause your child to be ridiculed and made fun of. This is something that can and should be prevented with proper education.

Improper education about this could even lead to your child being victimized by a pedifiler. If your child's staring at someone they may interpret in a different way that your child didn't intend. As you can see here the context and complexity of using the public restroom is a lot more intense than using our private restroom at home.

Using the urinal properly is an adaptive skill that must be learned. In the example above you can see how there are several micro steps involved in learning how to use the urinal properly. I will contest to you that with every adaptive skill there is come many micro steps to learning that skill. The thing that makes this hard for us to teach is that the micro steps tend to come naturally for neurotypicals. This makes it difficult for them to explain in detail all of the micro steps involved here.

My mind is able to process most skills in several many steps. I've found that I am able to think in micro steps in every occasion accept for when practicing social skills. This has been very frustrating for me. People constantly tell me how smart I am and I do feel like I'm pretty intelligent when it comes to physical skills. But when it comes to practicing social skills I don't feel very smart at all and become scared. Personally it's extremely frustrating to know that these social relationships come much easier for most.

I have to work twice as hard at socializing to even get close to where most people are at. But it's worth it. Hard work pays off.

I want to break this process down even simpler for you to understand. In this example we will use the metric system. We're going to refer to neurotypicals as centimetres. We'll refer to myself as a millimetre.

For this particular situation we will be asking someone for their opinion on a movie. In order for us to fully accomplish the skill we must move from 1 centimetre to 2 centimetres. In my experience I've learned that most neurotypicals could be instructed to go ask someone for their opinion about a movie and they would walk right up ask for the opinion, maybe engage in some small talk about the movie and then come back. The entire conversation and question usually happens in a minute or two tops.

I have to break this down and analyze it on a much smaller level if I'm going to do it properly. Without providing intervention and analyzing what I'm about to do I would walk right up to the person ask them what they thought about a certain movie and said okay, thank you and returned back to home base. Almost like a programmed computer asking someone a question. In order for me to avoid that type of interaction I must quickly analyze the upcoming social situation.

Let's take a look at the skill of getting a girlfriend. There's so much more to it then seeing a woman you're attracted to and approaching her to ask her to be your girlfriend. Seeing her is point A. Asking her to be your girlfriend is point Z. There are many other steps in-between A and Z. As someone on the spectrum I tend to go straight from A to Z in everything I do in life. This is where I have a huge problem of coming on too strong. I have often overwhelmed people and caused them to feel uncomfortable around me because I wasn't able to see the social boundaries that are established in relationships. These boundaries are what you would go through from point B to Y in order to get to the end goal or point Z.

So here is a real life example for me. I'm at a restaurant leaving. I see a woman sitting at a table that I like. Within about 2 seconds of seeing her I end up at her table and sit down with her. I'm already breaking several social rules. This girl was scared for her life because a random stranger approached her and just sat down at her table. I sat down before I even said hi. She had no idea what was going on. These are the exact words that came out of my mouth "Hi, I'm Travis, will you be my girlfriend?" That was four years ago. That situation didn't go very well and the girl ended up getting up and left the restaurant. It was an uncomfortable situation for both of us.

This occurred because I went from point A to point Z. I look back and laugh at it now because I've learned a few steps between A and Z which have improved my quality of life tremendously. I can't stress to you enough how much I believe in getting Applied Behaviour Analysis (ABA) therapy for people on the autism spectrum. I personally didn't learn anything about socializing from talking to a psychologist. I learned a little bit from talking to a few peers but the bulk of what I learned has come from reading about ABA or talking to board certified behaviour analysts. The sooner we can start a child on ABA the better their chances are of succeeding and having a successful life that they can be happy with.

Here's a look at how I should have approached this girl. Understanding context of situations better now I should have examined the situation thoroughly. This is where the ability to understand body language and micro expressions from facial cues becomes valuable. You first need to see if she is with a group of people or there by herself. If she's with a group of people does she have a boyfriend? The easiest way of doing this is to look for a ring. Sometimes that isn't possible. It's necessary to read body language between people to tell what kind of friends they are.

If it turned out she was there by herself then it would have been okay to approach her. I would have needed to walk up casually in a friendly way that said I just wanted to say hi but I'm not going to stay long. One thing I should definitely avoid doing is sitting down next to the person. It's inappropriate to invite yourself into a social group. It is definitely overstepping boundaries to sit down without even saying hi to the group.

Before asking for her to be my girlfriend there are several steps to take. Once I sit down I shouldn't just say. Will you be my girlfriend? I have been able to learn some of these steps by applying behaviour analysis on myself. I have self-reinforced with one of my favourite snacks "Chocolate Milk."

Asking her to be my girlfriend isn't a step that should be taken on the first meeting. So I have to tell myself to be patient and wait. I then need to engage her in small talk and allow her to talk about myself. I should also be paying close attention to social cues she is giving me throughout this entire process. If she's closing off then I should take the cue of her not being interested and excuse myself. If she is welcoming the interaction then I could proceed with getting to know her. Keep in mind that every person will be different. Some may welcome meeting new people and some won't. This is why we have to look at different contexts.

In teaching the skill of approaching someone it's best to teach it in several different contexts.

This skill should be taught in some of the following places.

restaurant

Bookstore

Coffee shop

Library

Mall

Grocery Store

Outside (the park, the street)

Work

School

There are a lot more places you could find to teach this skill. However, the rules to approaching someone to introduce yourself vary from setting to setting. This is something that someone on the autism spectrum will likely not naturally understand.

I want to give you an example of how complex a skill is here. In order to get a girlfriend I'll show you steps that need to be taken.

In order to get a girlfriend he will start with working up the courage to say hi, then saying hi, then engaging in conversation, then offering to buy a drink, then, asking for her phone number. Even to get the first date he will take 10 smaller steps in order to get there.

•Ex. 1 "Hi, I'm Travis, how are you today?"

•Engage in small talk

•Read body language

•Find common interest

•Build rapport

•Connect

•Ex. 2 "Hi, I'm Travis, can I buy you a drink?"

•Introduce yourself (Example 1)

- Read body language

- Find common interest

- Engage in Small Talk

- Build Rapport

- Connect

- Talk for more than 10 minutes

- Ask if she wants to dance

- Ask questions about her

- Find out what kind of drink she likes

- Buy her a drink

- Ex. 3 "Hi, I'm Travis, can I get your phone number?"

- Introduce yourself (Example. 1)

- Read body language

- Find common interest

- Engage in small talk

- Build rapport

- Connect

- Talk for more than 20 minutes

- Ask if she wants to dance

- Ask questions about her

- Find out what kind of drinks she likes

- Go to a deeper level to form stronger connection

- Buy her a drink after you know she's interested in getting to know you. (Example 2)

- Ask her for her phone number

- Ex. 4 "Hi, I'm Travis, will you have dinner with me?"

- Introduce yourself (Example 1)

- Read body language

- Find common interest

- Engage in small talk

- Build rapport

- Connect

- Ask her if she wants to dance

- Ask questions about her

- Find out what kind of drinks she likes

- Offer to buy her a drink (Example 2)

- Ask her for her phone number (Example 3)

- Call her to talk on the phone

- Text back and forth for a few days

- Ask her to go to dinner with you

Pay attention to how in each step I want to go from introducing myself to getting to the end goal. Also pay attention to how these examples come together as layers. This means that example's 1, 2, and 3 should typically occur before proceeding to step 4. There are four what I call macro steps. These are the big steps that you would need to take before asking a woman to be your girlfriend.

In between each step there are micro steps or sub steps. The micro steps are in italic print.

You can see how complex this is. There are a lot of steps to the process. It's not something that can be learned from peers. It's important to apply concepts of applied behavior analysis. I feel very passionate about using ABA for myself but also making sure other kids are given access to ABA growing up and as young adults.

Applied Behaviour Analysis (ABA) is science that involves using modern behavioral learning theories to modify overt behaviours. As an adult with Asperger's Syndrome this is a theory that I find useful to practice in my own life. It's extremely challenging to self-reinforce. I apply ABA to social situations so I can learn adaptive skills and function better in those areas.

I often run into people, some of whom are in the Autism community, who say ABA is not applicable to people with high functioning Autism or Asperger's Syndrome. I respectfully disagree with this opinion and have personal experience to back it up.

I tend to exhibit some classic Asperger's Syndrome traits like coming on too strong with people and being overbearing. I do this by texting or communicating with an individual too often. This behaviour is not readily accepted in our society; there are unwritten boundaries set in getting to know someone. This behaviour can cause people to be uncomfortable around me; therefore it is one that I have to change.

Without access to services as an adult I have had to be creative and come up with some of my own ideas for intervention. I'm not a therapist but I do have the knowledge of understanding how my mind thinks and works. This has allowed me to come up with strategies for changing my own behavior. I know neurotypicals (people who are not on the Autism Spectrum) who use the science of ABA on themselves every day.

When applying ABA principles I have to remember a quote from Dr. Peter Gerhardt, which states "Context is king." It is not possible to just sit in an office and work on one social skill for an hour or two and expect to be able to walk into any social situation and use the skill correctly.

Confidence and self esteem

If we do not meet our goal of educating our children about sexuality and puberty issues we run that risk of our children being made fun of or even taken advantage of. We must act now, not later. Every child with a disability needs to be able to express themselves. I have went through really down times in my life because I wasn't able to put these basic adaptive skills to use to be able to help fulfil my wants and needs. If we're unable to express ourselves on any level our happiness will fade away. The ability to communicate means everything. We have to keep looking at the ability to communicate as more than just the ability to speak. Communication is accomplished through several avenues and outlets. I recommend all teenagers on the autism spectrum have access to create their own private journal and even post it online for the public with a parent proofreading and monitoring comments and posts about it. This is another way for those of us on the autism spectrum to voice our frustrations and share our successes and attain social interaction via comments and discussion of the blog.

Once our self esteem fades we'll face the greater challenge of dealing with depression. I think with early intervention of ABA therapy and good education on puberty and sexuality we can lower the risk of our children experiencing depression symptoms as they become teenagers and young adults. Being educated will allow your child to be included in the group and be able to voice his or her opinions on all these subjects. Unless you plan to shelter your kid throughout the rest of his or her life they are going to encounter situations where sex is being discussed by their peers. Most of the time this happens at school. Not preparing your child because you don't know how is one thing but not preparing your child because you aren't comfortable discussing the issues with your child is another. We shouldn't be embarrassed to talk about our sexuality. We need to talk about it to ensure safety for our people on the autism spectrum.

Boasting from Peers

As important as it is for us to educate our own children on the issues of sexuality it is equally important that we make our people aware that what other kids say may or may not always be true. I have a personal story of my own to provide as an example here.

I had been so frustrated for such a long time. I was in my early 20's and I hadn't had any positive interactions with women. I desperately wanted a girlfriend. I was spending a lot of money buying books. I bought 5 or 6 different books on the subject of dating and relationships. I found these books by searching on Google.

We need to be careful of this. It's another example of what your child might do to find the information they are trying to access if they can't access it from the parents. I bought the books and read them and some stuff made sense most didn't. I hired a personal dating coach of my own and that was expensive. I purchased 3 or 4 different DVD Series on talking to women. I spent a lot of money trying to figure this stuff out.

One weekend evening I was at a club by myself trying to meet people when I met this guy. He was talking to me and we started discussing the issues of dating and relationships. I ended up opening up to him which I shouldn't have so soon. I told him I was having trouble talking to women and wanted to learn. I mentioned how I'd spent all of this money trying to buy DVD programs and books to tell me how to get a girlfriend. He thought that it was crazy I was spending so much money so he offered to help me out.

He told me to send all of those books and dvd's back and try to get my money back. I spent about $8,000.00 on books and DVD series in less than a year. He told me to get that money back and he'd let me hangout with him and his friends on weekends. He said he could show me how to get any girl I wanted. He told me he'd allow me to hangout with them if I paid him $500.00 per month.

This opportunity seemed better to me than paying thousands of dollars for books and dvd's. So I did it. This guy told me that he had been with over 250 girls and could get anyone he wanted and he'd teach me how to get any girl I wanted too. I was thinking "I don't want 250 girls I want 1." Here's a guy who's bragging about being with 250 woman and I can't even get 1. I don't want more than 1. Just 1 is all I need. We hung out for about 4 or 5 weekends in a row and then I ran out of money. But during that time I didn't learn anything. He told me in order to get a girlfriend I needed to be drunk when I was out. Liquid courage is what he called it. Needless to say I received a lot of bad advice that was actually counterproductive to what I was trying to accomplish. But because I wasn't able to access help in this area of my life from a correct source I began to seek out my own help. It was unhealthy. Knowing what I know today, I know the chances are that guy was probably way over exaggerating that number of girls he'd been with.

The above is just an example of how someone on the spectrum can go down a wrong turn quickly if we don't intervene and provide the social skills coaching and sexuality education from a young age. The goal is to avoid the wrong turns by providing the information at an early age so they can build upon that as they get older. We must continue to strive for early intervention. There is always room to take one of our kids further. We should never be content with where we're at. Push them further and see the results and successes they have.

I hope you have found this book helpful in understanding the way your child's mind might process information regarding friendships. Please remember to teach them the difference between a friend and a bully. Happy friendship making!

How I See God in Autism

ABOUT THE AUTHOR

Travis is 28 years old, turning 29 at the end of March 2014. Life has been challenging due to having autism and mental illnesses that are related to Autism. Schizophrenia is a scary thing. When a person hears voices or sees things that others don't it is very difficult to lead a normal life and function normally.

Schizophrenia much like Autism interferes with a person's ability for form and maintain meaningful friendships and relationships in life. Both Autism and Schizophrenia create significant social barriers that must be overcome. This book was written in hopes of helping parents who have children going through some of the similar issues to have someone to relate to. It's also for those people who have autism or have a mental illness of some kind and just do not feel like anyone understands them.

The process of getting help is daunting on its own. I just now have found a counselor I can confide in at the age of 29 who I feel is helping me with autism and schizophrenia. I've spent 7 years seeing over 100 counselors and several doctors who just could not understand what was going on.

I have a few amazing friends now and am thankful for that. This book will give the reader a look at how Autism and Mental Illness can be related. While we cover it a lot in the book it is important to note that Autism is not a mental illness by itself however autism may very well be masked by a mental illness such as Schizophrenia. People suffering from Autism and mental illness need your help, love, and support. Hopefully in reading this you are able to offer them that support and love by understanding what they might be going through just a bit better.

Travis Breeding

Printed in Great Britain
by Amazon